Honey Bees

by Lola M. Schaefer

Consulting Editor: Gail Saunders-Smith, Ph.D.

Consultant: Troy Fore, Executive Director,
American Beekeeping Federation

Pebble Books

an imprint of Capstone Press
Mankato, Minnesota

Pebble Books are published by Capstone Press
818 North Willow Street, Mankato, Minnesota 56001
http://www.capstone-press.com

Library of Congress Cataloging-in-Publication Data
Schaefer, Lola M., 1950–
    Honey bees/by Lola M. Schaefer
    p. cm.—(Honey bees)
    Includes bibliographical references and index.
    Summary: Simple text and photographs introduce the body parts of honey bees.
    ISBN 0-7368-0231-2
    1. Honeybee—Anatomy—Juvenile literature. [1. Honeybee. 2. Bees.] I. Title.
II. Series: Schaefer, Lola M., 1950–   Honeybees.
QL568.A6S28   1999
595.79'9—dc21   98-40909
                                                                       CIP
                                                                        AC

Note to Parents and Teachers

The Honey Bees series supports national science standards for units on the diversity and unity of life. The series also shows that animals have features that help them live in different environments. This book describes and illustrates the parts of honey bees. The photographs support emergent readers in understanding the text. The repetition of words and phrases helps emergent readers learn new words. This book also introduces emergent readers to subject-specific vocabulary words, which are defined in the Words to Know section. Emergent readers may need assistance to read some words and to use the Table of Contents, Words to Know, Read More, Internet Sites, and Index/Word List sections of the book.

Table of Contents

4

Honey bees are insects.

6

Honey bees have six legs.

Honey bees have hair.

eyes

Honey bees have large eyes.

proboscis •••••▶

Honey bees have
a proboscis.

antennas

14

Honey bees have antennas.

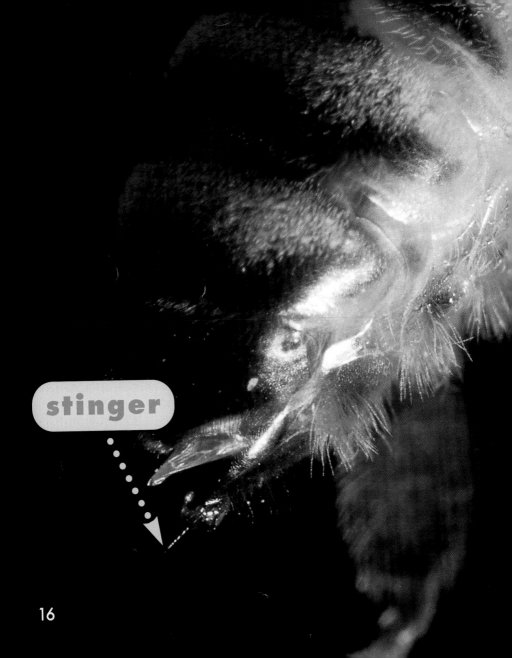

stinger

Honey bees have
a stinger.

Honey bees have wings.

Honey bees fly and buzz.

Words to Know

antenna—a feeler on the head of an insect; honey bees use antennas to smell, feel, and taste.

buzz—a humming sound made by flying insects; honey bee wings beat about 200 times each second; this makes a buzzing noise.

hair—small, soft strands that grow on the body of an animal; honey bees use hair to feel objects and to collect pollen.

insect—a small animal with a hard outer shell, three body parts, six legs, and two antennas; insects may have two or four wings.

proboscis—a part of the mouth that honey bees use for eating; proboscises are long and shaped like tubes.

stinger—a sharp, pointed part of an insect used to hurt enemies; honey bee enemies include bears, spiders, birds, and toads.

wing—a movable part on an insect that allows it to fly; honey bees can fly up to 22 miles per hour (35 kilometers per hour).

Read More

Crewe, Sabrina. *The Bee.* Life Cycles. Austin, Texas: Raintree Steck-Vaughn, 1997.

Fowler, Allan. *Busy, Buzzy Bees.* Rookie Read-About Science. Chicago: Children's Press, 1995.

Holmes, Kevin J. *Bees.* Animals. Mankato, Minn.: Bridgestone Books, 1998.

Internet Sites

Bee Alert!
http://www.umt.edu/biology/bees/trivia.htm

Bee Basics
http://www.roctronics.com/BEE-BASE.HTM

Bees
http://ezra.mts.jhu.edu/~naomi/insects/bees.html

B-Eye
http://cvs.anu.edu.au/andy/beye/beyehome.html

Index/Word List

antennas, 15
buzz, 21
eyes, 11
fly, 21
hair, 9
have, 7, 9, 11, 13, 15, 17, 19
honey bees, 5, 7, 9, 11, 13, 15, 17, 19, 21

insects, 5
large, 11
legs, 7
proboscis, 13
six, 7
stinger, 17
wings, 19

Word Count: 41
Early-Intervention Level: 4

Editorial Credits
Martha E. Hillman, editor; Steve Weil/Tandem Design, cover designer; Kimberly Danger and Sheri Gosewisch, photo researchers

Photo Credits
Charles W. Melton, 18
Dwight R. Kuhn, 6
James H. Robinson, 4, 8, 12
McDaniel Photography/Stephen McDaniel, 10, 14, 16, 20
Michael Habicht, cover
The Wildlife Collection/Charles Melton, 1